W9-AFY-475

SAVING ENDANGERED ANIMALS

By Jilly Hunt

capstone

© 2018 Heinemann Raintree
an imprint of Capstone Global Library, LLC
Chicago, Illinois

To contact Capstone Global Library, please call 800-747-4992, or visit our web site www.mycapstone.com

Edited by Adrian Vigliano
Designed by Philippa Jenkins
Original illustrations © Capstone Global Library Limited 2018
Illustrated by Oxford Designers and Illustrators
Picture research by Morgan Walters
Production by Tori Abraham
Originated by Capstone Global Library Ltd

21 20 19 18 17
10 9 8 7 6 5 4 3 2 1

Library of Congress Cataloging-in-Publication Data
Library of Congress Cataloging-in-Publication Data is available on the Library of Congress website.

ISBN: 978-1-4846-4140-8 (library hardcover)
ISBN: 978-1-4846-4144-6 (paperback)
ISBN: 978-1-4846-4148-4 (eBook PDF)

This book has been officially leveled using the F&P Text Level Gradient™ Levelling System.

Acknowledgments
We would like to thank the following for permission to reproduce photographs: Alamy: Nick Hanna, 19; ASSOCIATED PRESS, 20; Capstone Press: Philippa Jenkins, map 17, 21, 24, 26, ipad 11, 13, 15, 16, 23, 24, 26, 28, 32, 41, 42; Getty Images: Joel Sartore, National Geographic Photo Ark, (biologist) Cover, Mark Wilson, 23, MyLoupe, 22; iStockphoto: predrag1, 7; Newscom: DADANG TRI/REUTERS, 34, Jonathan & Angela Scott/NHPA/Photoshot, 12, niushupei EPN, 11; Shutterstock: Abeselom Zerit, 15, Ahturner, 10, AleksSafronov, 25, Alexey Seafarer, 35, Andrea Izzotti, 37, Anton Jankovoy, 17, arrowsg, 8, Birdiegal, 32, Brian E Kushner, 38, David Osborn, 5, Eugene Lu, 30, JB Manning, 14, jgolby, 31, Khoroshunova Olga, 43, Kjersti Joergensen, 36, konmesa, 27, KRISS75, 6, mary416, 41, Matthew Orselli, 39, Sergey Nivens, 1, snapgalleria, 4, Verochka L, 18, watcharapong06, 13, wavebreakmedia, 40, WitR, (leopard print) Cover, design element, worradirek, 29

We would like to thank Michelle Fournier, Interpretive Naturalist, Chippewa Nature Center, Midland, MI, USA, for her invaluable help in the preparation of this book.

CONTENTS

Some words are shown in bold, **like this**. You can find out what they mean by looking in the glossary.

Chapter 1

WHAT'S BEYOND THE HEADLINES ABOUT ANIMAL CONSERVATION?

"THOUSANDS OF GEESE DIE AFTER LANDING ON POLLUTED WATER"

"GIRAFFES FACING EXTINCTION"

"ELEPHANTS KILLED FOR IVORY"

We've all seen headlines like these about wild animals. But how much do we really know about these issues?

Wildlife is at risk from environmental changes and from human activity. When the number of animals in a species becomes low, we say they are threatened or at risk of **extinction**.

Why Does It Matter If Animals Become Extinct?

We need to look after all animals because they all have a place in their **ecosystem**. An ecosystem is a community of plants and animals that interact with each other. To understand how ecosystems work, we must understand food chains. A food chain is the link between plants, the animals that eat the plants, and the animals that eat these animals. Food chains can be different lengths. Food webs are many food chains connected to one another.

Food Web

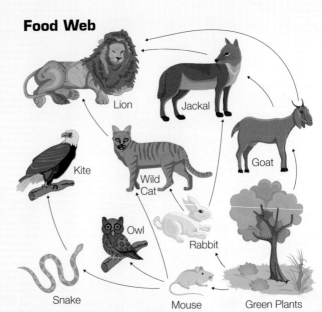

Lion

Jackal

Kite

Goat

Wild Cat

Owl

Rabbit

Snake

Mouse

Green Plants

Broken Chains

When an animal or plant disappears from a food chain, it can have drastic consequences. For example, in the 1930s, the gray wolf was killed off in Yellowstone National Park in the U.S. This turned out to be good news for the elk but bad news for the beaver. The wolf was one of the main predators of the elk and once the threat of the wolf was removed, elks thrived. However, the elk ate more than their fair share of the willow trees that Yellowstone's beaver population relied upon. The reduction in the beaver population meant fewer dams and ponds, which had an impact on the streams and water in the area. Fish in the area suffered and songbirds no longer had the same willow habitat to live in. When the gray wolf was reintroduced into Yellowstone in 1995, the ecosystem slowly returned to normal.

DID YOU KNOW?

Scientists know of about 2 million species of animals but they estimate there could actually be 5 million to 100 million different species living on Earth.

What Are the Biggest Threats?

The most common threat to wildlife survival is the loss or **degradation** of their habitats. Degradation is when a habitat is damaged. Loss, or degradation, of a habitat is usually due to human activity, such as clearing land for agriculture, removing trees for logging, building transport routes, building houses or other developments, energy production, and mining.

Pollution

Pollution can come from a variety of sources such as chemicals, oil, or trash. It can have an immediate impact on some wildlife and an indirect impact on others. An oil spill from a tanker at sea, for example, will affect the environment in a number of ways. The immediate impact is that animals in the surrounding area become covered in oil and die. The oil washes up on beaches and affects wildlife there. The affected environments will be unsuitable for plants and animals to live in. Pollution can also have an indirect impact by affecting how much food there is available or affecting an animal's ability to reproduce.

Deforestation is one type of habitat degradation.

Overexploitation

Humans also cause a threat to the survival of some animals by overexploitation. This is when too many of a particular kind of animal are hunted, fished, or poached. Sometimes certain animals are deliberately targeted. For example, elephants are known to be at risk for extinction, but poachers can make money from selling their ivory so they still hunt them. Many species of fish are at risk because humans have overfished them and have not allowed time for their populations to increase again. Also, during fishing, some fish and other sea creatures, such as turtles, are caught up in nets and killed unintentionally.

Climate Change

Climate change also affects the animal population. Increasing temperatures affect the food available to migrating birds, for example. Animals' ranges are also changing as southern species are shifting north to find the cooler temperatures.

Oil spills can do serious harm to animals.

How Do We Know Which Animals Are at Risk?

The Red List of Threatened Species is an international database that lists more than 79,800 species of plants and animals. This vital list is maintained by the International Union for Conservation of Nature (IUCN), which is a group made up of governments and other organizations. The Red List contains information about each species' range, population size, habitat and ecology, use and/or trade, threats, and conservation actions needed. The Red List groups plants and animals according to how at risk of extinction they are.

With an estimated wild population of about 400, the Sumatran tiger is critically endangered on the Red List.

Red List Levels of Risk

Category	Examples
Extinct	Ridley's Stick-insect
Extinct in the wild	Scimitar-horned oryx
Critically endangered	Black rhinoceros
Endangered	Asian elephant
Vulnerable	Giraffes
Near threatened	American bison
Least concern	Arctic fox

If species are in the critically endangered, endangered, or vulnerable categories, they are known as 'threatened' species. If action is not taken to protect these threatened species, it is likely that the species will die out. Species move into different categories on the list as their population changes. There are 7,978 **vertebrate** species and 4,338 **invertebrates** species that are listed as threatened. Scientists think that at least 38 species of mammal have become extinct since the list was begun in the 1960s.

Controlling Trade in Wildlife

Around the same time as the Red List was established in the 1960s, it became clear that the world needed a way to control the trade in wildlife that was putting so many plants and animals at risk of extinction. The Convention of International Trade in Endangered Species of Wild Fauna and Flora (CITES) was therefore established. This international agreement between the world's governments helps ensure that international trade in wild animals and plants does not lead to their extinction.

DID YOU KNOW?

- 41 percent of amphibians are threatened
- 25 percent of mammals are threatened
- 13 percent of birds are threatened

And these are just the species we know about. There could be species going extinct without us even knowing about them.

GOOD NEWS

Many species on the Red List have been saved from extinction. The gray whale, for example, was hunted to almost extinction in the early 1900s. International protection was introduced in 1947 and the gray whale population has since increased. They are now classed as "least concern."

Chapter 2

WHAT'S BEYOND THE HEADLINES ABOUT HUNTING AND POACHING?

Since ancient times, humans have survived by hunting. Today, humans still hunt to feed themselves but some also do it for sport. It is thought that humans hunting for food have caused the extinction of the great auk (a seabird that lived in the North Atlantic), the Atlantic gray whale and, more famously, the dodo.

Legal Hunting

In most countries, legal hunting has strict rules in place. There are controls over what type of weapons can be used and the user needs to hold a licence for these weapons. There are also rules about what types of animals can be hunted and when, and how many animals can be hunted during one season.

Legal hunting is regulated by the government. ▼

Illegal Hunting

Illegal hunting is also known as poaching. This is when hunters illegally take or kill animals. Poachers do this because there is a lot of money to be made. There is a global market for animal products such as ivory from elephants, horns from rhinos, and skins from many animals. Some animals are killed for their supposed **medicinal** qualities. Some people also want to keep exotic animals, such as snakes and chimpanzees, as pets or use them for entertainment.

Chinese authorities sort through confiscated ivory.

THINK ABOUT IT

Hunting has been making headlines because many people are concerned about animal welfare and believe that hunting is a cruel sport. However, hunting organizations do actively take part in animal conservation and many people believe it to be necessary in controlling the numbers of certain species of animal. What do you think?

Fighting the Poachers

Poaching is big business and is often run by criminal groups. Illegally selling wildlife is a major source of criminal earnings, coming only third behind arms smuggling and drug trafficking. The rewards are so great that wildlife criminals are willing to break international laws and risk fines and even imprisonment. Often, while those who are on the ground poaching are caught, the crime keeps happening because those leading the criminal gangs aren't.

A Kenyan game warden discovers a poacher's snare in a national animal reserve.

Many types of monkeys and primates are harmed by being sold illegally.

Rangers, Poachers, and Corruption

Countries have rangers in place to try to prevent poaching and there have been numerous successes. But there is also a lot of corruption, with the risk of rangers or law enforcement officers being bribed, and stories of light sentences for poachers who are caught. Criminals will often go where the animals they hunt have the least protection. This makes preventing illegal hunting difficult. The people doing the poaching may be local people with no job opportunities and no money. They may see poaching as a way of feeding their families. In some places, such as in Gabon and Cameroon, arrested poachers tell how they faced beatings or worse by poaching gangs if they came back without any animals.

Professor Lee White, the director of Gabon's National Parks Agency, says the situation is at its worst.

"People we arrest quite openly tell their story. In two-thirds of cases they were either employed or forced by the Cameroon military to join a poaching gang."

What Is Being Done About Poaching?

Organizations such as the WWF want to deter people from poaching by making it harder and riskier for criminals to do, and by making the rewards from poaching less attractive. WWF is working with the **United Nations** and CITES to put global rules in place to fight wildlife crime. Changing consumer behavior is also important. If no one wants to buy illegal wildlife products, then the poachers will stop.

Anti-poaching Work

The WWF wants to work with countries and their anti-poaching teams to offer training and the most up-to-date technology to help teams keep ahead of the poachers. Once caught, it's important that poachers are effectively prosecuted so they don't go back and do it again.

GOOD NEWS

In October 2016, China and the U.S. announced plans to close their ivory markets.

▲ A park ranger monitors sea turtle eggs on a beach in Texas. Sea turtles and their eggs are threatened by poachers around the world.

Getting Communities Involved

Getting the support of local communities is important in the fight against poaching. Local people can help alert rangers to the threat of poachers. If the community can see value in protecting their wildlife, then it will become harder for poaching to take place. Tourism can help local communities out of poverty, for example. A 2016 study found that elephant poaching was costing African countries about $25 million per year because of lost tourism. The study argues that investing in the protection of Africa's elephants would cost less than the money countries lose from reduced tourism.

THINK ABOUT IT

Kelvin has a small farm near the Lower Zambezi National Park. He works hard all day but at certain times of the year, when the elephants are hungry, he gets no rest. He must scare the elephants away before they eat all of his crops. How do you think someone like Kelvin would feel about protecting elephants from poachers?

Rhino Success

Rhino horns are used in traditional Asian medicines because they are believed to treat conditions such as epilepsy, fevers, stroke, and cancer. Although the effectiveness of these medicines has never been medically proven, it has led to a demand for rhino horns. Many rhino species are classed as extinct in the wild or at risk of extinction because of excessive poaching.

Zero Poaching

Nepal has shown that it is possible to beat the poachers. With enough resources and lots of hard work, they have achieved zero poaching. The warden of the Chitwan National Park puts their success down to keeping patrols working for 24 hours a day. The Nepalese Army played a key role in supporting the park rangers, providing 1,100 men and more when needed.

In 2005, Nepal's population of its threatened one-horned rhino was down to only 375. But as a result of Nepal's hard work, their rhino population is on the increase, with 645 recorded in 2015. With the hard work of rangers and the army, Nepal introduced tougher punishments for poachers. Park rangers formed close links with local communities to gain their help and support. Projects to encourage wildlife tourism were set up and locals received one-third of these revenues.

Prince William at a wildlife conference in Vietnam:

"Ivory is not something to be desired and when removed from an elephant it is not beautiful."

CHINA

NEPAL

INDIA

BHUTAN

Nepal

India

Indian
Ocean

resident rhinos

reintroduced rhinos

Visitors observe protected rhinos
at Nepal's Chitwan National Park. ▼

Poacher Arrested

In January 2015, a notorious poacher who had been living in Chitwan was caught. He was found to be responsible for killing 20 rhinos and injuring five. He was given a 15-year prison sentence to show other hunters that poaching is a serious crime.

GOOD NEWS

In November 2016, the President of Tanzania ordered a crackdown on elephant poaching. This led to the arrests of a significant number of poachers and also to the confiscation of 50 pieces of ivory.

Chapter 3

WHAT'S BEYOND THE HEADLINES ABOUT OVERFISHING?

Overfishing happens when people catch more fish than nature can replace. It is a big problem for both the fish population and for people. Billions of people eat fish as their main source of protein and millions of people depend on fishing to earn their living. Scientists predict that if humans continue fishing at current rates, by 2048 all the world's fisheries will have collapsed. There will simply not be enough fish left to support future fishing.

Many governments around the world are trying to improve regulations in order to protect global fisheries.

DID YOU KNOW?

The world's fishing fleet is thought to be up to two and a half times the size that is needed to catch the fish that we actually need.

How Did This Happen?

Overfishing started in the early 1800s, when people destroyed the world's whale population with their demand for blubber for lamp oil. By the mid–1900s, humans had fished Atlantic cod and herring and California's sardines almost to extinction. In the 1950s, governments offered incentives to increase fishing as they looked for an affordable, protein-rich food. This led to a more industrial way of fishing, as big businesses replaced the local fishers. The fish population became out of balance, especially since people tended to fish for the larger species such as southern bluefin tuna. The effect of overfishing predators like this is that food webs and ecosystems change.

What Is Being Done About Overfishing?

Strict limits over the number of different species of fish have been put in place to help fish populations recover, but illegal overfishing still happens. The Marine Stewardship Council (MSC) was set up to help consumers identify which fish have been caught in sustainable fisheries.

Certification labels from groups such as MSC help consumers make sustainable choices. ▶

DID YOU KNOW?

In 1989, 90 million tons of fish were caught—that's the same weight as 50 million cars!

Marine Protected Areas

One way of trying to rebuild the world's fish population is through marine protected areas (MPAs). These protected areas give habitats a chance to recover. Indiscriminate fishing using nets and traps can unbalance ecosystems. For example, the removal of algae-eating fish unbalances a coral reef ecosystem. Destructive fishing practices are not allowed within MPAs. There are also no-take zones where fishing is not allowed at all. These zones offer protection for other sea creatures too, such as the endangered sea turtle, that is at risk of getting tangled up in fishing nets and drowning.

Researchers discovered one of the largest sponges ever in an MPA off the shores of Hawaii.

Increasing MPAs

In May 2016, U.S. President Barack Obama expanded an existing MPA off the coast of Hawaii to create one of the world's largest marine reserves. The Papahanaumokuakea Marine National Monument will now cover about 582,578 square miles (1.5 square kilometers). That's twice as big as Texas and six times bigger than the United Kingdom! Conservationists were keen that the MPA be expanded following the discovery of over 100 new species in the area. These included a giant sponge that is about the size of a minivan and could prove to be the oldest animal on earth. The reserve will protect more than 7,000 marine species, including whales, sea turtles and yellowfin tuna.

The First International MPA

In October 2016, officials from the European Union and 24 countries agreed to create the world's first marine reserve in international waters, which will be in the Southern Ocean around Antarctica. Within the park, there will be an area about the size of France and Spain combined where no fishing can be done at all. This is a really important zone because scientists think that the Southern Ocean is where three-quarters of the nutrients in the rest of the world's oceans come from.

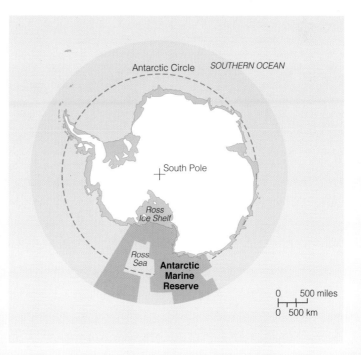

The Antarctic Marine Reserve will cover more than 579,153 square miles (1.5 million sq km) of ocean.

An End to Overfishing in U.S. Waters

In the 1990s, the fishing industry was feeling the impact of decades of overfishing. In 1992, the New England ground fishery had gone from having a plentiful supply of cod, haddock, and flounder to collapsing and being declared a disaster by the U.S. president. By 1996, 86 species of fish were classed as overfished. This was bad news for the oceans and bad news for the people who depended on fishing for their living.

U.S. fisheries, such as those in ▲ New England, are important for local economies.

Putting It Right

The U.S. needed to put restrictions in place to try to rebuild fish stocks and end overfishing. They introduced fishing laws that would help rebuild the fish population as quickly as possible. There were rules about the type of fishing gear allowed and permits were issued to control the number of fishing vessels. Zones and time periods were established where fishing couldn't take place. Scientists created plans to manage overfished stock and limits were set on how many of each species could be caught. The limits on how many fish could be caught changed, depending on the scientific data about the fish population. It is thought that the flexibility of these limits is why the laws were successful. The limits could be reduced if the fish population wasn't increasing as quickly as expected.

On January 6, 2009, ▲
U.S. President George
W. Bush moved to
protect a massive area of
the Pacific Ocean by creating
new conservation areas.

DID YOU KNOW?

By 2016, 64 percent of the fish stock covered by the laws had been rebuilt.

THINK ABOUT IT

These U.S. fishing laws haven't been as successful in supporting fish that migrate, such as sharks and tuna. Conservationists are calling for similar laws to be introduced around the world. Do you think this would be a good idea? Or do you think that each country should be able to make its own rules?

Chapter 4

WHAT'S BEYOND THE HEADLINES ABOUT HABITAT LOSS?

The biggest threat to wildlife is habitat loss. The Red List identifies habitat loss to be one of the main threats for 85 percent of the world's threatened species.

Once again, it is human activity and need that is causing this problem. Forests are being lost because of the harvesting of timber and wood for fuel, and because people need more land to grow crops or graze cattle. It is thought that around half of the world's original forests have been lost.

areas of forest

present areas of deforestation

This map shows the places most at risk of deforestation.

THINK ABOUT IT

Scientists think that tropical forests contain at least half of the Earth's species and yet at least 42 million acres (17 million hectares) of tropical forest are being cleared each year. What will happen to these species? What about species that scientists haven't yet discovered?

Natural habitats are also being lost due to mining as humans try to extract the precious resources from under the Earth's surface. Pipelines and roads are built to support mining activities. Industrial developments and housing also cause more pressure on natural habitats. Unstable governments and wars can affect habitats and wildlife populations.

What Is Being Done About It?

Conservationists, such as the WWF, believe that creating protected areas is one of the best ways to conserve animals. They believe that a well-managed protected area, such as a wildlife reserve, can also benefit the local community by providing job opportunities, water supplies, and food supplies. The International Union for Conservation of Nature (IUCN) represents more than 100,000 protected areas around the world.

DID YOU KNOW?

Orangutans have been victim to human activities. Their habitats in Indonesia and Malaysia are rapidly disappearing and the orangutan is at risk of extinction in the wild.

Category	Description	Example
1. Strict nature/ wilderness area	For wilderness protection or science	• Denali National Park and Preserve, U.S. • Great Victoria Desert Nature Reserve, Australia
2. National park	For ecosystem protection and recreation	• Yellowstone National Park, U.S. • Mu Ko Ang Thong National Park, Thailand
3. Natural monument	For conservation of unique natural features	• Natural Bridges National Monument, U.S. • Ganga Lake Natural Monument, Mongolia
4. Habitat or species management area	To maintain habitats and protect species	• Central Kalahari Game Reserve, Botswana • Kawau North Cove, New Zealand
5. Protected landscape or seascape	To protect landscape or seascape and recreation	• United Kingdom national parks • Minnesota Valley National Wildlife Refuge, U.S.
6. Managed resource protected area	For the sustainable use of natural ecosystems	• Lake Hefner, U.S. • Annapurna Conservation Area, Nepal

Doubling Wild Tigers

Wild Tiger Populations by Country, 2016

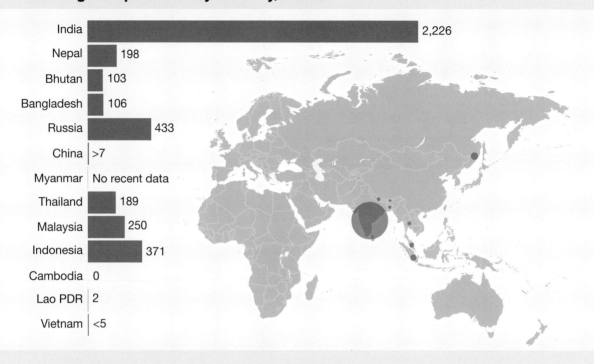

Country	Population
India	2,226
Nepal	198
Bhutan	103
Bangladesh	106
Russia	433
China	>7
Myanmar	No recent data
Thailand	189
Malaysia	250
Indonesia	371
Cambodia	0
Lao PDR	2
Vietnam	<5

The tiger is an endangered species and experts believe that if the threat of habitat loss and the risk of poaching continues, the tiger may completely die out in the wild. Conservationists estimate that only 3,890 tigers exist in the wild and that the world's population of wild tigers has decreased by 97 percent since the beginning of the 1900s. Three tiger subspecies, the Bali, Javan, and Caspian, have already become extinct.

India's Prime Minister Narendra Modi:

"Tiger conservation is not a choice, it is an imperative."

Ambitious Aims

The WWF has a campaign to try to double the world's population of tigers by 2022, which would see at least 6,000 tigers living in the wild. This is an ambitious global aim. The WWF are supporting tiger countries to carry out research and surveys to find out more about their tiger populations. They're training the local wildlife rangers to do these surveys and to help ensure the protected areas are properly managed. The WWF are working with local authorities and communities to help those people living in tiger territory to live alongside the tiger. The good news is that in 2015, India's tiger survey showed that their population had increased from 1,706 in 2010 to 2,226 tigers. This means that India now has over half of the world's population of tigers! This increase in tiger numbers is due to improved protection, better management, and more tiger reserves.

GOOD NEWS

In Russia, a new national park was created in 2015 which provides more protection to the endangered Amur tiger. On the Indonesian island of Sumatra, 100,000 acres of rainforest was granted protection. This is not only excellent news for tigers but also orangutans and elephants.

Human-Wildlife Conflict

Experts estimate that there are 7.4 billion people living in the world today. As the human population grows, people build homes in natural areas and farm larger areas of land. This expansion can reduce animal territory and can bring humans into conflict with animals. For example, in Nepal the greater one-horned rhino is blamed for destroying crops, and tigers are blamed for preying on pets and livestock if their natural prey is scarce. Humans may even be killed by some wild animals. Locals naturally want to defend their territory, their crops, their lives, and that of their livestock. Many animals are killed to stop future conflicts, even though the wild animal population might be endangered.

Innovative Defenses

In Botswana, different approaches have been tested to try to keep wildlife out of conflict with humans. Elephants don't like the smell or taste of chili peppers so people have tried building chili pepper plant fences. This also has the benefit of providing an extra income from selling the chili peppers. Elephants also stay away from bees so a fence made out of beehives was tested and proved to be successful. Training people so that they can find work with tourists who want to see the wildlife also helped to change people's viewpoints about wild animals.

THINK ABOUT IT

In Africa, the people most affected by these human-animal conflicts are usually very poor farmers with small farms. An animal the size of an elephant could destroy such a farmer's whole crop in one night. Is it acceptable for an endangered animal to be killed if it is causing damage to humans? Or should other ways be used first?

▲ Conflict between elephants and humans is a serious threat to the animals. It is important that humans continue to find ways to address these problems.

Urbanization

Experts predict that by 2050, two-thirds of the world's population will live in urban areas, and that urban settlements will cover more than 115,830 square miles (3 million sq km). That's about the size of India!

Roads can have the effect of cutting off areas of habitat from one another. This can disturb the balance of an ecosystem.

All this urban development has a big impact on wildlife. For example, just building a new road can cause many conservation issues. The road can cause an immediate loss of habitat as land is cleared to build the road. There will be noise and land pollution during the building of the road. When the road is finished, it acts as a boundary and breaks up an animal's territory. Animals are squeezed into a smaller area, which might lead to conflicts with other animals. The road brings humans closer to the natural environment and could lead to conflicts. Roads provide a fast route in and out for poachers of large animals. Humans may also use these roads to bring non-native animals into the area. These new animals compete for space and food. They may even bring in new diseases that the existing wildlife are not protected against. And, of course, there is the danger a busy road brings to humans as well as wildlife.

GOOD NEWS

The Wildlife Trust in the United Kingdom are working with landowners and other organizations to reconnect areas of woodlands and wetlands allowing wildlife to travel freely.

CASE STUDY:

Giant Panda

Glyn Davies, the executive director of global programs at WWF, said this in 2016 in reaction to a significant increase in giant panda populations:

"This is a cause for celebration and proves that a united approach can bring a substantial difference to threatened species."

The Wolong National ▲ Nature Reserve in Sichuan Province helped protect an area of habitat for pandas.

In the 1980s, it looked like nothing but bad news for the giant panda as the species seemed to be heading for extinction. Conservationists estimated that there were fewer than 1,000 pandas living in the wild. Poaching and deforestation were responsible for this sad decline of the symbol of China. The Chinese government needed to take immediate action, which it did. It became tougher on the skin trade which had been providing a market for the animals caught by poachers. It established the Wolong National Nature Reserve in Sichuan Provence in 1980.

In 2002, the government began a project to reforest 5 percent of China—an area about three and half times as big as the United Kingdom! This was an ambitious task but one that would have many benefits if successful. The re-creation of the country's forests would help prevent soil erosion, droughts, and floods. It would also reduce the effects of dust storms. Within this reforestation plan was the creation of further nature reserves for pandas and China's other endangered wildlife. There are now 67 nature reserves which help protect about two-thirds of the wild panda population.

On the Increase

The really great news is that the population of wild giant pandas are starting to recover and numbers are increasing. In 2004, the wild panda population numbered 1,596. Ten years later, this figure had increased to 1,864 pandas.

DID YOU KNOW?

Conservation efforts are having a positive effect on the panda population. But the giant panda is still classed as vulnerable on the Red List. Climate change is a further threat to pandas. Scientists warn that climate change may cause the loss of the panda's favorite bamboo habitat in the next 80 years.

Chapter 5

WHAT'S BEYOND THE HEADLINES ABOUT POLLUTION?

Pollution can take many forms—smog from traffic fumes, **noxious** gases from industrial processes, **pesticides** running into rivers from farmland, trash trapped in a hedgerow, or a plastic bag floating in the ocean. Pollution can be from a local source such as a farm or a factory but it can also travel for thousands of miles. Pollution can affect all living things in an ecosystem, even humans, because everything is linked.

This may look more like a landfill site but it is, in fact, the Citarum River in Indonesia. The area's textile factories discharge their wastewater containing toxic chemicals into the river, killing off fish and other wildlife. Many local fishers have turned to plastic recycling to earn a living.

Toxic Chemicals

In many ways, modern lifestyles are reliant on the use of chemicals. However, many of these chemicals are toxic pollutants that can travel large distances. Some are absorbed into our bodies or the plants and animals that we eat, or even the water that we drink. One of the dangers of these toxic chemicals is when they build up in the food chain. Plants and smaller animals absorb these chemicals. Larger animals then eat them, and therefore absorb more of the chemicals. The amount of toxic chemicals builds up and up in the food chain. Top predators, such as tuna, are often the most affected by this kind of toxin build-up. These toxins can cause diseases, birth defects, and **genetic mutations.**

It's Too Light

Light pollution is the orange glow that towns and cities have at night when lights are on. Light pollution is confusing animals. For example, birds use the moon and the stars to navigate on their migration routes. When these birds reach a town or city, they get confused by the extra lights, with sometimes the whole flock flying into over-lit buildings.

Baby sea turtles hatch almost in unison and then rush to the sea together. This behavior increases their chances of surviving waiting predators. ▼

Light pollution at night is also putting the lives of endangered sea turtles at risk. When baby sea turtles hatch, their natural instinct is to follow the bright light of the moon to guide them to the relative safety of the sea. Instead, light from coastal developments takes them in the wrong direction and puts them at an increased risk from predators.

Noise Pollution

Noise pollution, created by humans with our busy urban lives, vehicles, and factories, is putting wildlife at risk. It is interfering with the way animals communicate, breed, and hunt. Some species of bat have been found to avoid crossing over busy roads, which fragments their natural hunting grounds and reduces their habitat.

DID YOU KNOW?

Oil and gas exploration in the Arctic causes increased underwater noise and more sea traffic, which is disturbing the feeding and breeding of belugas and bowhead whales.

GOOD NEWS

Florida has some important nesting sites for the sea turtle. In the 1990s, local governments became stricter at enforcing cut-off times for certain light sources. They also implemented a change in light bulbs to a type that doesn't disturb turtles as much. These light pollution changes, combined with other conservation efforts, have helped the number of turtle nesting sites to increase dramatically.

Bald Eagles

The bald eagle is a symbol of the U.S., but just 50 years ago it was in danger of extinction, with only 487 nesting pairs left in the wild. The bald eagle was blamed for preying on livestock, so many farmers shot them down. In 1940, a law was introduced to help protect the species. This made it illegal to kill, sell, or possess a bald eagle. But eagle populations continued to struggle. By 1966, the southern subspecies of bald eagle was listed as endangered.

DDT

▲

In 1942, the Swiss chemist Paul Hermann Müller discovered an artificially produced chemical which could control mosquitoes and other insects. This pesticide was known as DDT. It seemed like good news and totally unrelated to the survival of the bald eagle (and other birds of prey).

In addition to conflict with humans, bald eagles also suffered from habitat loss and degradation.

The bald eagle population in North America is now estimated to be about 70,000.

Impact of DDT

As with other pesticides, DDT washed into rivers and waterways where plants and fish absorbed it. The bald eagle ate these contaminated fish and the poisonous chemicals entered the eagle's body. DDT affected the shells of the eagle's eggs and made them weaker. The eggs often broke or just didn't hatch, which affected the population of eagles that was already at risk.

The dangers of DDT became known in the 1960s and in 1972 the use of DDT in the U.S. was banned. In 1978, the entire population of bald eagles in the U.S. was declared to be endangered.

The good news is that the wild bald eagle population has increased. The DDT ban, a captive breeding program, nest site protection, and law enforcement efforts have all helped eagles. The bald eagle is no longer classed as an endangered animal.

GOOD NEWS

Professor Carl Jones, a biologist from Wales, is credited with saving nine species from extinction! In 2016, he was awarded the Indianapolis Prize and said he is proud of this award as it recognizes the importance of conserving all animals, not just the "megavertebrates," because all animals play an important role in an ecosystem.

How Can We Make a Difference?

Perhaps you think of animal conservation needing to happen in the grasslands of Africa or the tropical rainforests of Brazil. The threat of habitat loss, pollution, or conflict with humans can affect animals much closer to home too.

We can all play a part, from thinking about the actions we take to trying to influence the actions others take. We can do simple things like switching off outdoor lights to try to minimize light pollution. We can find out more about these issues and tell friends and family about them. The more people who know, the better. We can be proactive and join campaigns run by global conservationists. We can support groups such as WWF or Greenpeace that let world leaders know that wildlife needs to be conserved.

◄ Anyone can get involved with local conservation efforts. Perhaps you could join an effort to clean up a park, nature reserve, or even just your school's grounds.

As consumers, we can shop carefully and only buy sustainable seafood that is MSC-certified. There are over 20,000 MSC-labeled products sold in 85 countries, so there's plenty to choose from! We can check labels to ensure that products use sustainably produced ingredients.

◀ The endangered red panda is just one of many species around the world that need help from conservationists.

THINK ABOUT IT

Anyone can help animal conservation efforts. Eight-year-old Carter Ries and his seven-year-old sister wanted to do more than just "adopt" an animal. So in 2009 they set up their own charity called One More Generation, or OMG, which raises awareness for endangered species. For example, they've started a letter-writing campaign asking people to write to Indonesian president Joko Widodo to encourage his support in protecting orangutans in Indonesia.

Conclusion

Human activity is the biggest threat to animal conservation. Climate change, loss of habitat, pollution, and poaching are all putting the lives of animals around the world at risk. If an ecosystem collapses, it can have major consequences for the humans who live in it, as food and water supplies can be severely affected. There are also potentially millions of undiscovered species and who knows what humans may be able to learn from them. There might be a species out there that can provide humans with clues of how to prevent killer diseases such as cancer, or even just how to stop the common cold.

There are still too many critically endangered species that need protection. The wild mountain gorilla population, for example, is down to only 880. Humans need to consider the effect on ecosystems when expanding industrial, urban, or agriculture developments. We need to persuade people to think about the consequences of items they buy, and persuade governments around the world to support zero-tolerance poaching schemes. We have seen that with international effort we can be successful. We just need to continue our efforts.

Dr Robin Freeman of the Zoological Society of London:

"But one of the things I think is most important about these stats, these trends are declines in the number of animals in wildlife populations—they are not extinctions. By and large they are not vanishing, and that presents us with an opportunity to do something about it."

GOOD NEWS

New conservation techniques have been tried and proven to be effective. For example, the controversial technique of ecological replacement has been shown to work. On islands in Mauritius, the Aldabra giant tortoise was introduced to replace the original Mauritian giant tortoise which had become extinct. The replacement tortoise filled the gap that had been left in the ecosystem by performing similar tasks such as spreading seeds in their droppings. This has helped rebuild the whole ecosystem.

TIMELINE

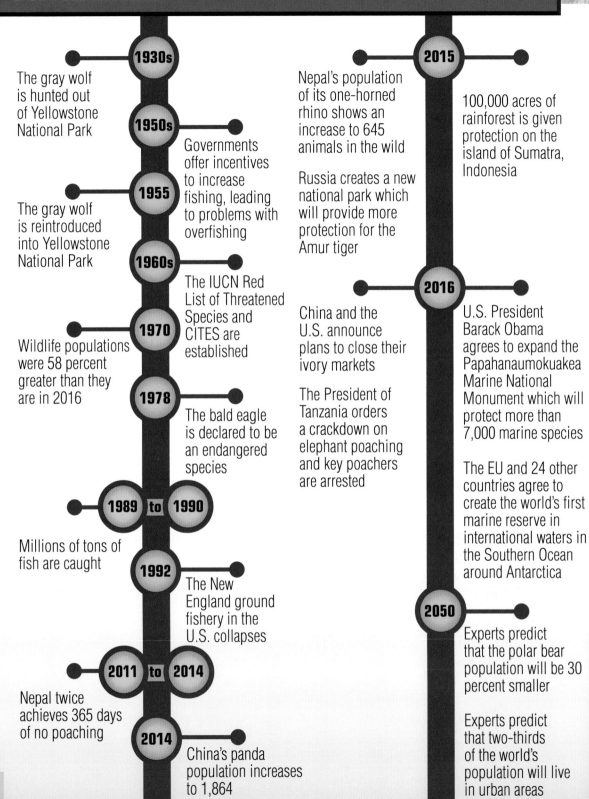

1930s
The gray wolf is hunted out of Yellowstone National Park

1950s
Governments offer incentives to increase fishing, leading to problems with overfishing

1955
The gray wolf is reintroduced into Yellowstone National Park

1960s
The IUCN Red List of Threatened Species and CITES are established

1970
Wildlife populations were 58 percent greater than they are in 2016

1978
The bald eagle is declared to be an endangered species

1989 to 1990
Millions of tons of fish are caught

1992
The New England ground fishery in the U.S. collapses

2011 to 2014
Nepal twice achieves 365 days of no poaching

2014
China's panda population increases to 1,864

2015
Nepal's population of its one-horned rhino shows an increase to 645 animals in the wild

Russia creates a new national park which will provide more protection for the Amur tiger

100,000 acres of rainforest is given protection on the island of Sumatra, Indonesia

2016
China and the U.S. announce plans to close their ivory markets

The President of Tanzania orders a crackdown on elephant poaching and key poachers are arrested

U.S. President Barack Obama agrees to expand the Papahanaumokuakea Marine National Monument which will protect more than 7,000 marine species

The EU and 24 other countries agree to create the world's first marine reserve in international waters in the Southern Ocean around Antarctica

2050
Experts predict that the polar bear population will be 30 percent smaller

Experts predict that two-thirds of the world's population will live in urban areas

GLOSSARY

climate change—a significant change in Earth's climate over a period of time

corruption—willingness to do things that are wrong or illegal to get money, favors, or power

degradation—a decline to a condition of lower quality

ecosystem—a group of animals and plants that work together with their surroundings

extinction—the state or process of becoming extinct; an extinct animal is one that has died out, with no more of its kind

genetic mutation—a change in an animal's genetic makeup that causes it to develop in a different way

incentive—reward or payment that motivates someone to do something

invertebrate—an animal without a backbone

ivory—the natural substance of which the tusks and teeth of some animals are made

medicinal—having healing or curing qualities; used as a medicine

migrate—to travel from one area to another on a regular basis

noxious—toxic; hazardous to health

pesticide—poisonous chemical used to kill insects, rats, and fungi that can damage plants

United Nations—a group of countries that works together for peace and security

vertebrate—an animal with a backbone

FIND OUT MORE

When finding out more about conservation issues, remember to think about the reliability of the source. Does it have an interest in persuading the reader to think in a particular way? Sometimes only certain information may be presented so the reader doesn't gain the full picture of an issue.

National news websites, newspapers, and journals such as *Nature*, are a good way of keeping up-to-date with the latest information about environmental issues.

Internet Sites

Use Facthound to find Internet sites related to this book.

Here's all you do:
Visit *www.facthound.com*

Just type in 9781484641408 and go!

Read More

Gogerly, Liz. *Caring for Animals.* Charities in Action. Chicago: Heinemann Raintree, 2013.

Hunt, Jilly. *The Environment.* Beyond the Headlines. Chicago: Heinemann Raintree, 2017.

Kalman, Bobbie. *Why and Where are Animals Endangered?* New York: Crabtree Publishing Company, 2015.

Langley, Andrew. *Saving the Environment.* Charities in Action. Chicago: Heinemann Raintree, 2013.

INDEX